poetically preserved

A Book of Poetry and Musings

COURTNEY LUCAS

ISBN: 978-0-578-79442-6

Poetically Preserved

Proudly self-published through Divine Legacy Publishing, www.divinelegacypublishing.com

To my 3 heartbeats- Madison, Kailyn, and Jade.

You are forever loved.

-Mommy

For every soul that has found themselves in darkness,
searching for the light.
For every burden you've silently carried so that everyone else
would be alright.
For those who are healing from the pain of their past and the
terrors of the night.
For those who sometimes feel like life has given you much
more of a load than you can take.
For those who are surviving the snares of evil, refusing to bow,
bend or break.

This is for you.

Table of Contents

The Rose — 2

Passion	3
The Sky	4
Father Wound	5
Truth	8
Family	9
Emergence	11
Sorrow	13
King	14
Come Out	15
No Doubt.	17
Shame Free	19
Offense	21
Glorious Skies	22
Love Letter to Me	23

Reclaim — 25

Freedom	26
Self-Reflection	27
Israel	33
Overcome	35

Holy Ground   37

Worship   38

Believe Writing   39

True Warriors   40

The Wilderness Writing   41

Lessons...   42

Falling   43

False Value   44

Frenemie   45

Journey On   46

A-1   47

Trust   49

Snake   50

Married Men   51

Free   52

Repeat   52

Raw and Uncut   53

Ruling Fear   54

The Package   55

Real Writing   56

Unfolding   57

All   58

Misunderstood Writing   59

Differences   61

Opinions   62

Sleep…	63
Free	64
Hypocrisy	65
Above All	66
Trailblazer Writing	67
Going Through	68
Others	69
Givers	69
Box	70
God is God	71
Never Alone	72
Protected	72
Straddling	73
Culture	73
All Things	73
Shackles	74
Inferior	74
Black Man	75
HATE	77
To my Brother…	80
Cycles	82
Wounds	82
Absence	82
Secret Place	83
Whispers	84
Father Healing	85

Choices 88

Ava 89

Catapult 90

forgive yourself 92

Tears 93

Grief Calling 93

Exhaustion Writing 94

Self Care 95

Healing Writing 96

Young, Single Mothers Writing 97

Pure 99

How 99

Voice 100

Deuces 101

Steps of a Mother 102

To My Mothers 103

Self-Motivation 104

Careful 105

Life Goes On... 106

Everything is Everything 106

High Road 107

To Win 108

Wonder 109

Cowards 110

Love Known 111

A Flower 111

Honor Thyself 112

This Moment 112

Scam 113

Holding Writing 114

Distracted Terrain 115

Wreck Yoself 115

Potential 116

Expired 116

My Addiction 117

Disguised 118

The Maze 119

Soul Snatcha 121

Intuition 123

A Collection of Hearts 125

Perception 126

No Convo 126

Over 127

One Day 128

Released 128

Mistake 129

Self-Loyalty 130

New Lane 131

Femininity 132

Reclaim 133

Healing love 135

More 135

My Love 136

I Do 137

The Beauty of Trust 138

I Felt Love Today 139

The Rose

When no one even cared

The rose it grew from concrete

Keepin all these dreams

Provin nature's laws wrong

It learned how to walk without havin feet

It came from concrete...

You see you wouldn't ask

Why the rose that grew from the concrete

Had damaged petals

On the contrary

We would all celebrate its tenacity

We would all love it's will to reach the sun

Well, we are the rose

This is the concrete

And these are my damaged petals

Don't ask me why

Thank God...

Ask me how

-2 Pac, Nikki Giovanni

Passion

Crouching tiger, hidden dragon.

Tell me now, where lies your passion?

I want to see, hear, and feel - Don't hinder your light.

There's no time for masking.

Stand bold. Stand confident. Stand sure.

Knowing that you possess all it takes to endure...and endure
you will!

One day, one moment, one step at a time.

But it must first begin with the elevation, exploration, and the
expression of your beautiful mind.

Generate goodness - not calamity. This world has many things
to offer.

You'll emulate what you choose.

In this life, you will continually gain, find, and lose.

Above all else, grab your potential off the shelf.

Take joy in honoring yourself.

Be sure you make your mark on this world in your vast, yet
limited, amount of time. So, when you make an exit, you can
look and say, "The pleasure was all mine."

The Sky

I told my daughter if you ever forget, just look to the sky.

She looked up at me and asked, "Mommy, why?"

I told her that it serves as a constant reminder in this
broken world and illusion of human power that, even
when life gets sour,

the same God who created this is the master of your soul.

Find strength in knowing that he is in control.

Just as the clouds pass by, so will you, so will I.

To say you won't be sad or upset would be a lie.

There are plenty of days the sun won't shine, and the
clouds will cry... But you must keep on moving - life's a
constant dance.

And remember, as long as you're able to see the sky, you
have breath, life, and a chance.

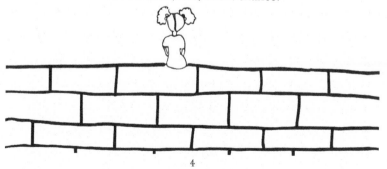

Father

The feelings of being...good but not good enough.

Loved but not loved enough.

Unique but not special enough.

Not enough to remember or enough to call.

Not enough to support, nor to show your love through action

at all. Trying to believe that my worth is far more than rubies

in a land where none finds me worthy...the irony of that.

I've longed for you...I waited for you.

You planted these dreaded flowers in my garden, and

everyone strolling after you has stopped to glance and catch a

view yet seem to water them the same way you do.

Sparse and sparingly...

I have not the heart to kill your plot in hopes that you shall

one day return to it and see that I held on to the hope of you

because it is you I have loved. Endless proving that I can be a

good girl, Daddy; I can make you proud.

I will sit down nicely, do whatever you say.

I'll serve you. I'll stay out of the way.

I'll even play blind to your anger and mistakes; I'll be quiet.

See? I have nothing bad to say as long as you'll stay.

Daddy, please don't go.

I'm told I have such a beautiful smile. You've said it too.

I know it's the time I look the most like you.

So, I can't help but wonder when you look in the mirror, do

Wound

you see me smiling back at you? The tears have stained my
face, my eyes are clouded, and I can't find my way.
Starting to really feel like a disgrace.
Because I've stumbled and fallen a few times, running so fast
in hopes to numb the past. So my dress, no, it's not white
anymore. And my heart, well, every time I think I've thrown
away the key, someone who resembles you knocks at the door.
I have denied myself over and over - my wants, my needs, and
my desires - no, they can't get in the way of the longing I have
for your embrace. So, I continuously search... I wait, I hope,
endlessly, that one day you'll come back to the little girl in me
and be all she believed you to be.
She will never give up on you, no not for a million years.
Through the struggles, the hurt, the shame, and the many
nights of countless tears.
It all comes back to you, and the hope I still hold on to, for
you to come undo the day you chose to walk right out of my
life. To undo this repetitive abandonment, rejection, and
strife. My heart is lonely. I hate this place.
Stuck here in this desert feeding on hopeless assumptions
and whys.... I've got to find a way to truly heal, accept, and
release in order to move on with my life.

Truth

Truth is not always pretty. Sometimes truth hurts.

When you've been sleeping within false depictions creating

the comforts of illusion, and the reality of truth awakens you,

you must see it as a blessing. Picture truth as the light being

turned on in a dark room of lies.

Fear will arise, betrayal will anger you, and the pain may

tempt you to hit a downward spiral.

But the truth, when harnessed, can set you free and the pain

will empower.

So, get up, dust yourself off, and close that door. Because

there is something you have to still hold on to, and that my

dear is your truth - the strength, beauty, and blessing found

within you.

family

You left me in my darkest moments...couldn't take my truth -
you didn't want it.

I'd always think about that moment when I told you,
you remained silent.

How could you condone it? The silence is ringing so loud in
my ear - can you not hear?

How can you not care? Over me you chose my molester.

Abandoning me in pain, you chose denial and kept her.

This mask is crumbling. I can no longer fake it...

In the name of "family", I can no longer take it!

The constant juggling of everyone's hearts in my hands.

I'm trying not to break my stride.

Loyalty is my specialty; in this, I put my pride.

Yet when it came time to stand for what was right, who
protected mine?

My heart is bleeding, feeling like I'm suffocating - I'm finding
it hard to want to keep breathing.

In the absence of the ones, you'd give it all for, family.

It seems life has no real meaning.

I've spent my life trying to build on top of cracks, standing unstable on a non-supportive foundation.

Learned behaviors of misconstrued arousals haunting me through the addiction of masturbation. Trying to run from it all, but my feet feel like they are glued.

Flashbacks & panic attacks. I want to wake up from this nightmare, but reality doesn't have a snooze. I'm finding it hard to maintain in my current situation.

Suffering with a disbelief in sincere love, and it's poisoning all of my relations.

What is family? I ask myself, seeking to create my own definition.

I vow not to become complacent in this place.

A new beginning healed and fulfilled is my ambition.

Releasing this nonsense, giving myself a new name.

I'm on a mission.

Emergence

I want to cry but a part of me just WON'T let me do it! It's the "victim" mode that wants to have its way and I am so tired of it. I am done! She keeps me in situations and cycles, places I shouldn't be in! Tolerating things and people I shouldn't just because of her fear. Fear of change, the future, loneliness, disapproval. Strolling with vulnerability – a constant display of naive, attracting like a sign that reads: "Welcome all with tricks up their sleeves." I'm so tired of it! I can't tolerate this and TRULY expect to go higher. She keeps me stagnant, silent, passive, accepting, and in denial. She's crippling me, yet she's all I've ever known, the one that was there when I cried every tear and self-understanding when I did wrong. So gentle with me but handicapping at the same time. I'm tired of suffering her fear, self-limitations, and the backwards truth she's accepted that are lies. Swallowing my identity in order to keep her alive. I'm ready to move on from here, from them. Yes, all those dead in relations and baggage I've accumulated from this empty yearning, from me. The part of me that is and has been my silent friend - who won't let me forget the betrayal, molestation, abuse, the words, the neglect, and the pain. I want to escape and live free.

How I would be, but she'd rather choose to see tomorrow
through yesterday's lens and find comfort in that which she
has always known - pain and insecurity she has made her
home. But I've got to leave her; this negativity is a drain.
The more I hold on to it, the more my life becomes a shame.
Pain on repeat like a wilted flower incapable of full bloom.
Potential on delay instead of reaching its peak.
In order to be all that I can be,
I have to make a decision to free me from me.

Sorrow

Hello, my name is Sorrow.

I know things you don't want to know.

I'm in places you don't want to go.

I'm the one you don't want to show.

I come along with the rain, resentment and pain. Causing you

to grow-higher than you are … and deeper than you'd like to

go. If you let me in,

I can be a miserable friend or your best motivator.

It's all depends on you – yes, hear me out.

My name is Sorrow, but I don't hold your tomorrow.

Truth be told, I want you to see that you do!

So, please push through.

Heavy as can be, I still lie at your feet.

I do not like this misery of basking in defeat.

As daunting as I may be, I long for the opposite of me.

To be in perfect harmony.

So, can you please find the strength to worship and put on

the garment of praise so your light can shine and brighten up

your days?

We must find ourselves out of this dark and hazy maze.

King

This love affair began a while ago when I was young, broken,
and helpless on the floor.

Hoping that someone would care enough to open up the door.

Crying out to you, I knew there had to be so much more than
dysfunction on repeat.

I pray you'd see, hear, and rescue me.

You did, and you still do, draw me nearer, closer unto you.

You touched me in a way that no one had before,

pursuing me with an infinite love so pure...who knew that this
love would endure?

Through all the many tests of time, I've remained yours,

and you have been my everlasting lover.

The friend that sticks closer than a brother.

The One who picked me up even when forsaken by my own
father and mother.

With you, who can compete?

And if you be for me, then who can be against me?

I rest in your shelter, your almighty hand.

To you I bow, for you I stand.

You are my everything.

Come Out

Once again, I find myself in this place shadowed by disgrace.

I've lost so much time in this masquerade,

trying to reveal her face.

We keep playing hide and seek as she withholds the depth of

her true beauty from me, but guess what?

I've already had a peek of the fullness behind the facade.

And although I have seen you naked and ashamed before God

-

His spirit allows me to see the true you before the impurities

and contaminations.

A vision that surpasses all condemnation.

Please, come out for a real conversation.

Baby, you don't have to stay in this dark damnation.

Who has convinced you that you must keep company with the

worst parts of your past?

This game could be over; can we make this our last?

Aren't you tired of being tickled by self-defeat?

Stand in your strengths; don't bow to playing weak.

Make yourself known and say what you need to say.

For there is a love that awaits to bring you out of the darkness

into a new day.

I'm here to tell you that you, my dear, hold his very sunshine.

You know how I know this?

Because you are mine, I love you.

Be willing enough to trust and give God room to work.

Have faith and take the humanic limits off of God.

Remember and hold strong to the absolute truth that He is able to do the exceedingly, abundantly, above all that we ask or think according to HIS power that works in us....

But first you must surrender, give him what you have in your hands.

Those limiting fears along with your deepest desires.

Sometimes we can be burdened down by doubt, worry, and the weight of "how".

We see what we have through carnal eyes and limited lens.

Curating a double-mindedness and stagnancy that keeps us from going forth.

Discrediting and viewing it as small, embarrassed, and ashamed at even having the thought at all.

God can use what you hold for His glory.

You doubt the vision, yet you saw it.

He revealed it to you and that glimpse continuously woos you like David and his slingshot, the widow woman and her oil, the boy with five fish and two loaves of bread, and Moses with his rod.

We must give it ALL to God and allow our faith to rise

up in order for him to multiply it, knowing that it is not by our power, nor our might, but by His spirit.

This requires you to be humbled, in full surrender, and continual solitude, faith, worship, and expectation.

Ephesians 2:10, "For we are God's handiwork, created in Christ Jesus to do good works, which God prepared in advance for us to do."

No Doubt.

Shame Free

Let it go.

Don't hold on to it.

You are to be meek. Release.

Stand still. Abide in me. Abide in love
and grace.

For I have graced you for this.

I will fight the battle for you.

Lay it down. Rest in me. In my peace that
passeth all understanding.

Focus in on me. Not them.

Not their mood, not their faces, or their
acts of distraction.

Victory is yours.

Their shame belongs to them. It does not
belong to you.

Do not pick it up. Refuse to play with it
or even acknowledge it.

You have been delivered from this, set
fully free from the burden of shame,
guilt, and disgrace.

It is not yours to handle, it is theirs. How
they choose to walk is up to them.

It has nothing to do with you. Grace and
mercy - love, freedom, and abundance
are your portion.

He will remove this cup from you and
cause you to forget the pain, shame,
reproach, abandonment, and rejection
of your youth.
I will give you full recompense and
multiplied restoration.

Offense

When unpacking shame, embracing pain, rises offense.

It's not that you don't have a right to be offended - you were violated, hurt, betrayed, wronged.

The issue is trying to move past it.

Offense keeps you trapped in a place of realized hurt, anger, pity, and pain.

It robs you of your peace.

I want to walk fully in love. No more wrestling with offense.

I want to have power over it, not let it have power over me.

There are times in life where you just have to learn to surrender and go with the flow because it's like a draining, useless, uphill battle to go against it. Knowing when is the biggest struggle. In the middle of the storm and waves, sometimes it's better to go with the flow instead of going against the current. We have to just surrender and trust that at the end of the wind, waves, stormy rain, and threatening thunder, we will rise and appreciate the fact that at the end of the day, no matter what has come against us, we have survived. We are able to lift our eyes . . . that no one or nothing has taken our lives. This, my dear, is the prize.

glorious Skies

Love Letter to me....

Rise up and experience a new love. A refreshed version of you that was buried deep down inside under the muck and mire. Underneath the mess she's been buried, trapped, and calling out to be unstuck, to experience growth; to be free. Like Cinderella or Ariel trapped and limited under the sea. Sleeping Beauty needing to rise and be free or more like Rapunzel desiring to release into all she could be. There's more to me, to you, and she's ready.

Come out, my dear; there is no fear. I promise to love and embrace and learn all there is to know about you. I will never doubt you. No more hiding your face. I've struggled, traveled years to find you, greet you, love you, remind you, that this - you and I - is home and this love will never go away. I've learned to love you properly. No longer mimicking what was taught to me and done to you, which distorted us. My life's purpose and mission will be spent in honor of you and in reach of girls and boys we represent.

So, let the remainder of this life be dedicated to the true beauty of who you are, Courtney Shantel, and the strength of the love you encompass.

You are truly amazing, and I am so proud to be you.

I apologize for the pain that's been caused and the damage that's been done. The times I sat back quiet when you became undone. When I should've stood up. Spoke up. No more silence. No more tainted love. All good and perfect gifts come from above, and that my dear is what you are deserving of. No more settling. Period. In friendships, love and relationships, business, self-development, home life, or family. God is calling you to a standard of excellence. Honorable relationships. You are deserving of good, healthy, loving, dependable, honest, trustworthy, quality relations who sincerely support and are genuine. Who love you - truly love you, and want you to win without deceit, jealousy, resentment - true honest friends.

Let the journey begin...

Reclaim

Let's explore the paths between the mind, heart, and soul - motivations and strongholds - in preparation for the journey that is left to unfold. In your hands you hold…the power of decision.

freedom

Break away and finally allow yourself to personal freedom.

Freedom no longer stifled by the lies of invalidation, the root

of insecurity, and the fears that attach through codependency.

The time and effort you've spent chasing grace, trying to fill

this space with people and things - not realizing you are your

own queen in a land where you must first be honored by your

recognition.

You alone are the answer - no one else holds the ammunition.

So, take this time to listen.

To put aside every weight and thing that so easily ensnares.

You're on a mission of celebrating you, making all you

desire to be true of following your ambition - you don't need

permission from anyone to be who you are meant to be.

And tell me what is lonely?

You are your first true friend and lover; that type of loyalty

can rarely be found in another.

Let's focus on development, the reclaiming of self and energy

spent. Say goodbye to the internal woes.

Smile at the parade of joy for your very soul...

You are a story waiting to be told.

THIS love is one unconditional, patiently waiting to unfold.

Rooted in you, it'll never grow old.

Self-Reflection

So...I'm looking in the mirror and who do I see?
It's my outer self staring back at me....

"What's up girl? What's the matter? I've been seeing you
walking around here looking sadder and sadder. I've already
told you there is no strength to be found in being meek!
People will walk all over you. You keep trying to be all sweet.
In this world, only the strong will survive. Your Inner Girl?
You'll be a fool to let her in. That's why she's buried deep
down inside. Leave it up to her, we'd never win. You know
me! I like to play it cool, so all that sharing, caring, and telling
'our life's story' is most definitely against the rules. Nobody
wants to play patty cake with all those emotions and painful
memories. You do know people use your weaknesses against
you in your greatest time of need. Besides, she just wants to
play victim, so can we not go there please? And I understand,
we grew up in church, I love God and to somethings I'd never
go back, but who you think you're psyching with this talk of
full commitment to him? Hold up, pump your breaks! Let's
take this a few steps back. Are you serious? We too young!

The rest of your life would be so wack. You know I like to dabble in a lil bit of this and a lil bit of that - and you're trying to bring me into subjection? Where they do that at? The church itself is full of drama. You can even ask your own Grandmama. People are so judgmental - constantly throwing shade - full of cliques, envy, and competition. Why would I want to be amongst the saved? Everybody's stepping on, under, and over each other. People so fickle; they'll even betray their own brother. Yet you still screaming, 'Love one another!' When you going to open up your eyes and realize it's every man for himself? While you're out here trying to save the world, it's detrimental to my health. Look, all I'm trying to say is through it all we must stay on fleek. So, put my game face on and keep that chin up; ain't nobody got time to be looking weak!"

"Okay, you've got a lot of good points, I guess you're right. It seems like I am losing this fight between good and evil. Maybe we are all just backward people. I give up! I'm never going to get it right."

But before I could even get out of sight, I felt a tugging at my heart.

"Look Inner Girl, before you even start."

"No, let me speak before you let her pull your card. Now, you know as well as I do that you have a purpose and all of this is not in vain. She's always trying to drown the truth out and upon everyone else she places the blame. By doing that you're giving away your power - making it impossible to change. How long will you deny this self-inflicted pain? Hellooo! I'm hurting here! This stuff isn't going to just up and disappear. You continue to leave me stranded in this box of gnawing insecurities and fears - as if they simply do not exist. The physical wounds may be gone, but I'm still hurting from the times he punched you with his fist. And how many times are you really going to try to drink me away? Don't you realize when you sober up the next morning, I'll be staring you in the face? And those 'friends,' I've tried to warn you about those girls, but you still insist! There are so many things we need to address; you just refuse to look at this list! When the Holy Spirit warns you, you really need to take heed. It's like you keep sticking a dagger in your own heart but get mad with God when it bleeds! You drag me here, you force me there, you know she's fake, but you don't care. You keep trying to fill this void; I'm so sick and tired of all this noise and nonsense chatter - so let's be clear about the matter. I've been with you since birth, from the very moment you began to breathe... I hold the innocence of you - before the damage left its sting. I value who you are; I know your purpose and who you came to be.

Please, in all you do, don't neglect your inner me. Outer girl, she wants to be conformed to the word...wearing a mask like a frenemie coupled with self-sabotage and destructive behaviors; yes, you can be your own enemy. I mean, look at the choices you make. It's like we're always a dollar short and a day late. Stop comparing your life and taking advice from all these phony friends. Quit pouring all the best parts of me into these lousy, no-good intentioned men. All of this crap you constantly take. Give me a break! None of these cover-ups serve as an escape. The only thing that makes me feel right is the righteous redemption I have found in Christ.

And how dare you belittle me for screaming, 'Love one another!' Even in betrayal - he's a friend who'll still closer than a brother. Vengeance is His. I don't have to hold on to strife. I function better in love. It is the fruit of my life. And as far as drama and wrongdoing in the church, newsflash: You're not in heaven; we're still amongst humans on earth! We've got to keep our mind set on higher things. Ignore the petty and focus on what's pure. Sin is everywhere, understand that Christ alone has the cure. See yourself through the beauty of His eyes. Take your focus off of Him, and you will continue being hurt. You can't look to people for what only he provides: unconditional love, acceptance, and endless worth. So, forsake not the assembling. Continue to worship; hate and division are two things we cannot afford to choose. Don't be enticed by the wicked ways of this world.

In Christ, there is nothing to lose.

Standing there, staring at myself in the mirror, I made the decision to honor my Inner Girl by making an effort to hear her. I asked God to forgive me and as my soul cried, a song I'd heard before came from deep within my spirit. As I felt the broken parts of me rise, I knew I needed to hear it. So, I opened my mouth and began to sing...

"Fill my cup Lord. I lift it up Lord. Come and quench this thirsting in my soul. Bread of Heaven, feed me til I want no more... Fill my cup, fill it up, and make me whole."

Wallowing in the guilt and shame.

Laying here gets you nowhere - it'll only deepen the pain.

You've passed the test, made beauty from mess.

But because you've fallen a few times along the way, you forget about the rest.

You've prayed, repented, forgave, and yes, God has blessed.

But, you wrestle with suppressed feelings of unworthiness that keep you from your best.

Self-sabotage at an all-time high; anything resulting in greatness you defy

because you have settled for the enemies' lie.

You know that there is a greater truth - you must continue to believe it when it comes to you like you have before - as you've asked, look around he's done a new work.

Things aren't the same; he's done the impossible: moved mountains on your behalf - shown

favor amongst those who counted you out and was your very backbone so that you could stand bold.

You don't have to fret when faced with the old nor suffer in the valley of self-blame.

O Jacob, God has given you a new name.

But you must know it! When faced with a reflection of the past, correct and show it who you truly are; the beautiful healing of those scars.

We rejoice in overcoming our struggles fought in the dark. And when day breaks, walk in the fullness of who you are...

Israel

Overcome

Alone...alone with my sin, I let him go. Mixed feelings, dull emotions...I can't cry.

I know what this is, what needed to be done, and the reason why.

So, here I am with this disgust needing to be cleansed, this emptiness longing to be filled,

this heart only wanting God's will,

and I'm trying to stir up faith with all my might to really believe that I'm winning this fight.

That all is not pointless, in righteousness, and in making a change from squandering his grace.

Taking one step and then another, learning to maintain this pace.

Some things seem easier said than done, took forever to do just one, but I took the step.

Now what, I ask myself? I'm trying not to look back, but the fear of regret and the unknown persist in making its attack.

Help me, Father. I need you now; yes, I'm feeling faint.

I expected a fresh joy, a new song, not to be left here feeling blank. Or maybe this is a part of the plan to see if I'm going to do what I can.

Faith in action, to pick up my bed and walk. I shall, I will decree it for the time is now.

Stand tall in who you are, strong one, to this sin you no longer bow.

This is to be celebrated - the power, beauty, and freedom sought after in this new space.

Honor it, praise God, and love on you; you just overcame a huge hurdle in this race.

Let the blood do its cleansing work, renew your mind, get before his face.

The joy of the Lord is your salvation and no one can take his place.

I am so proud of you.

Holy Ground

You have to get to a place of sacred determination and unshakable tenacity.

I'm not going to trade my blessing. I refuse to compromise His anointing and the power vested in me. I will guard my heart, my mindset, and all I choose to entertain. And from anything that contaminates or contradicts, I choose to refrain. I will protect this sacred space of sanctity and peace, free from all burdens, fear, and shame. A place where his presence rules overall.

Where his spirit purifies and quenches every thirst. Where without him, you feel like a fish out of water, so you understand that He must come first.

Fully consumed, you need him to sustain - nothing can compare, no one else can maintain.

A true encounter with the father, and your life will be forever changed.

One touch from him, and you will never quite be the same.

Above all else, over and over, His truth will remain.

Full armor. Protected. Powerful, in love…safe and sound.

Found basking in the glory of his presence.

This is Holy Ground.

Worship

When worship is the only thing that satisfies your longing.
Sometimes I just sit in silence and let my soul pour out.
There is no greater feeling than worship, communion with
the most high, and no greater space than that secret place of
surrender. Humbleness, repentance, purification, and silent
glories of restoration. He has given us the garment of praise
for the spirit of heaviness. Humble thyself before his mighty
hand. He is your strength and His eyes are always upon you.
He is the beginning and the end. He holds our hand, walks
with us in between.

Faithful is our God. Count on him to see you through and
rejoice today, for you shall recover it all. There is power in
your worship. My deepest cares I lay at your feet. You're always
making a way for me. Your love is always here, never out of
reach. Amongst the fears and the doubts. When I can't seem
to figure it out, worship is my escape, my passport into peace,
and my soul-filled sacrifice. My right in the midst of wrong,
it is my personalized melody throughout life's turbulent song.
Hallelujah. Worship is everything.

Believe Writing

We say we believe in God, that "He is able and with Him ALL things are possible" - yet we still get hung up on the negatives derived from others and within ourselves. If we believe or hope in God for ourselves, why do we limit his grace when it comes to others?

The Bible says that He is not a respector of persons. He loves you just as much as He loves your perceived enemy. It is His will that NONE may perish... Don't be selfish, unforgiving, or try to limit God's grace in doing so because all you're doing is limiting yourself. God moves in love not hate. We wrestle not against flesh and blood but against principalities and spiritual wickedness in high places. So, come up off of that pettiness and realize who the real enemy is. He knows that love conquers all. Without love, you have nothing at all. God is love and God flows through love, but if you choose hate, how can God operate? That's why the enemy stirs confusion, because he knows if he can harden our hearts it makes it hard for God to use it. Faith is the substance of things hoped for, the evidence of things not seen and as a man thinketh so is he. The word is showing that there is power in our thoughts and the way we choose to see or think of others and ourselves.

Put prayer and supplication into action and give it time to manifest, but all that negativity will do is contradict and delay the positive. Fear and faith don't mix. Speak life and affirm greater continually in faith. Give faith room to operate.

True Warriors

Emotional highs and lows can only take you so far. "Those that hunger and thirst after RIGHTEOUSNESS shall be fulfilled." It's a lifestyle change.

We must move beyond a spiritual walk of self-serving emotional fulfillment. We, as the body of Christ, need refreshed tactics that go beyond the faces of our church into the trenches of this world where spiritual warfare is rampage! A real famine. People are thirsty, starved of hope in righteousness, and spiritually dying! We must arm ourselves and become radical united warriors with a kingdom mindset in order to be truly effective. Come up off those temporary fixes and push forward out of your comfort zone to this combat zone.

The Wilderness Writing

"Let he who be without sin cast the first stone." I'll wait....
Stop shaming people just
because their sins are on display, and yours are not! There
are levels to this. You nor I may know the facts and mysteries
surrounding when, what, how, or why. What a person is
crying out to God about in the midnight hour or what the
thorn in their flesh maybe.

So, humble thyself before life does it for you. Besides,
somebody has to bare the testament of true deliverance;
someone has to go through some things to lengthen the
empathetic reach of ministry and understanding. Don't boo
from the sideline of someone else's life. Pray for that person
and let God work.

Lessons...

Some lessons are learned in tears. Embracing some lessons
takes days, months, even years...

falling

When you know there is a shifting, but you don't know in what way. And although you feel you should be praying, you know not the words to should say. Hmmmm....I bet there is a disconnect, and it's evident, this is heaven sent - a spiritual alert trying to keep you away from that hurt. Stay woke Lucas.

False Value

The wicked seek power through manipulation.

Selfish ambition is their ammunition.

Stay on guard. Pay attention to intentions; some desires are

rooted in exploitation. Let no one exploit you.

Wherein there is no desire to give, empower, or bless that

which is at stake but rather to taste, explore, plunder, and take

from the desirable thing they see with no intention to stay nor

respect to let it be. Their mindset is what can I get from you to

further elevate me?

When you operate out of a place of envy, competition, or

strife seeking to block someone's shine you ultimately get

in your own way by dimming the light. It's enough darkness

in this world. Choose to unite, ignite, and be the light.

Iron sharpens iron. Light helps us to see. I'll carry the

light for you, as you carry the light for me. So thankful

for Torchbearers; those who rise above the ego and get to

Kingdom Business

frenemie

Does it bother you that I'm unbothered?

That you backstab me and I come back harder? Fair-weather
friends, living off of comparisons.

As long as you're up, we can be down. I stay 10 toes deep,
always celebrating with my peeps!

But let that script flip, if it ain't through the act of pity, you
start to act real shitty.

Tell me, why must you always feel superior? Egotistic based
friendships. Guess I don't meet the criteria. Cause I'm here
for you in the good and bad. I cheer for you when you're
happy or sad. I held your secrets, guarded your fears, and
stood by your side down through the years.

But it hurts you to give a compliment, grieves you to praise,
and envy shows in your grin if I'm having too many good days.

I don't understand this dynamic - I've tried for so long to
give you the benefit of the doubt. The truth is it makes you
feel better about yourself when I am down and out. It saddens
me to know that you find more pleasure in my frown than to
have me stand next to you also wearing a crown. You don't
ride for me like I do for you. Sad, but it is true.

A pawn in your game...our definition of "friend" is not the
same.

Journey On

I know the way your heart is set up; you want to carry others with you. You want them to see, feel, and experience this shifting. But truth be told, we are on our own journey, developing in our own timing. Sometimes you have to go it alone and get it for yourself...and that's okay. It doesn't mean you love each other any less. It simply means that your journey is taking you to another level. What you must not do is become stagnant and deny yourself the growth in transitioning just to be comfortably uncomfortable. There is no such thing. It's a facade because you know better. You take the loss, playing it small in order to fit because you're not living up to your truth - the full potential of who you are. Don't allow doubt, fear, and uncertainty to cover it up by rejecting your true reflection and this greatness inside of you. Be courageous enough to stand tall, and honor all of who you are along with the vision of what you aim to be. Keep writing it, pursuing it, and believing it. No matter who comes or what goes. Dust yourself off, be relentless... Walk in it; it's yours. Accept your path fully and intentionally plan to journey on.

α-1

When you were the last to know or be invited to a party of lies featuring you....welp, surprise surprise. You could've at least given me the chance to refute. But it's okay, unlike you, the enemy I will rebuke. I guess when you detach and rise, leaving it all behind, you become oblivious to the den of lions, out of sight out of mind, but look me in my face, hear me when I say - No, thank you! I think I'll remain in my own space of truth, solitude, and grace. Y'all can have the lies, drama, and hype. There is so much more to life. It can be frustrating trying to maintain, staying in your own lane, focused on higher things. Then someone wants to play the game of blame in order to benefit their name, so upon yours they cast shame. Yet still I will remain. For in retaliation of my own, there is no gain. I serve one who sees and knows everything. Those who know me know I keep it 100 about who I am - flaws and all -my ups and downs, times I've dropped my crown. Queen NaEve (Naive), wore my heart on my sleeve, but I've learned many will deceive and transparency can leave you with a frown. You see, betrayal wears a smile.

You assumed they'll "hold you down" and they did that, just not the way you'd expect - from behind, right through your back. Ahh ha...But no need for attack because every cause has an effect. Just know that it won't go unchecked. Seasons and cycles, you'll learn to respect. I'll let God handle the rest for He knows what's best. Mercy unto you; my pure heart will forever be true. Took a few L's, but they were necessary lessons. Still standing here today. Counting it all as blessings.

Trust

Refuse to think negative or speak less of yourself. Only positive! There will always be someone there to do the opposite - who speaks negatively directly to you or indirectly about you. Leave the dirty work to them and let God work out the kinks, spots, and wrinkles. One thing about TRUTH - it always prevails, and it is always revealed. The Spirit knows the Spirit, and in the end, that is all that matters.

God sees all and knows all, from the darkest motive to the hearts purest intent. Trust.

Snake

The snake right in front of you that you don't see but has you

for no direct reason hating me.

Married Men

Don't send me messages, stop hitting my line. You chose your
wife. Now, do your time.

She has your all; why should I give you mine? Miss me with
those tired ol' lies. You coming at me sideways because you
heard once before I got out of line. Are you deaf? Can't hear?
Or am I supposed to be blind?

If she knew what you do, she'd lose her mind!

You vowed to sacrifice. I won't be used to coddle you.

Man up, pay the price - a cost you should give willingly:
a committed heartfelt reward of pure, sincere love and
integrity, therein which

you are the Head. Honor your covenant and your word. Yes,
all the things you stood at the altar and said. I shouldn't be in
the position of having to protect your marital bed.

Free

Free to feel how I feel, free to see as I see, free to speak
as I speak, free to fully be me.

Repeat

When it comes to life, risk, and vulnerabilities, traveling paths
that began to look like you've been down before. Don't fight
nor doubt yourself by allowing someone to tell you not to
compare and similarities to ignore. Or to entice you and deny
the lessons you've spent your very life learning.
It'll only leave you less and yearning. Take a stand for yourself
and say no more!
You are capable, my dear, to close that door.

Fighting unknown battles, masking unseen scars, drowning
in a heart of pain and lost in a sea of betrayal - he'll meet you
right where you are.
Be patient and gentle with yourself - healing is a process.

Raw and Uncut

I'm not taking on your bad attitude. I'm not taking on your shame. I am not your emotional trash can. I refuse to play this game. You need to take responsibility, or you will drive yourself insane.

If you never stop to be real and calculate what's causing your loss, how then shall you truly gain? You need to change your point of reference - your perception cannot be the same.

Look yourself in the mirror; you're the one to blame.

Now, my friend, let's work through the pain.

Ruling Fear

There is no peace where fear is present. You can't remain stagnant in fear of change and move forward in the peace of a new beginning at the same time. That's not possible. You have to step out on faith in order to give your desires the opportunity and space to manifest. Not making a decision is the decision to stay right where you are. Who holds the key to your elevation? You. Make the necessary changes.

The Package

One thing that irritates me is a woman so shallow to believe
that beauty is truly only skin deep. Who doesn't know or care
to do anything else but get a high off being cute.
There is so much more to life than looking the part;
how about BEING the part.
Contrary to what the media portrays, looks can only get you so
far. It may get you somewhere, but it won't keep you there. If
you're not secure enough to stand, compromise will be your
fall. True beauty: Being mentally, emotionally, spiritually,
physically, and financially healthy, creates the whole package.
No missing pieces.
Get it together.

Real Writing

Whether we like to admit it or not, at some point in time,
we've all had insecurities.

Some have learned to live with them, and others have learned
to overcome them. Some people cover them up with shallow
pride: Hair, makeup, and material things. Some choose to
displace it upon others by being envious, jealous, or hateful
because truly they're insecure within themselves, and then
there are people like me: transparent, humble, and often
viewed as weak yet not in denial about insecurity. I've learned
that in order to conquer anything it must
be addressed-even if you are a beautiful mess. Allow anything
that makes you feel insecure to always motivate you into
improving and becoming your best! In this, you will always
be independent and secure. Real recognizes real, and real
recognizes fake, too.

Unfolding

Sometimes, you're just not ready. Allow yourself the time you need to adjust, to realize, to release your soul to find the answers it needs and your heart to grasp the closure it takes your mind to accept whatever it is to learn in the in between.

This is time. This is journey.

This is life constantly unfolding.

all

I don't find strength in making others feel small. There are
many different flaws, weaknesses, and shortcomings.
Who has them? ALL!

There's an opportunity for ministry in every situation for
every person through everything. But it's up to us to adjust
our minds, shift our perceptions, and recognize the true
need. When we lean unto our own understanding, it adds
insult to injury; but, when we put ourselves aside and
see through His eyes, beautiful things happen, and He is
glorified.

Misunderstood writing

It's not easy serving others and being misunderstood - the root of unappreciation. It's hard trying to love and be accepted by others when all they can see is intimidation. Because of their lack of faith, inability to see, and unwillingness to embrace his greatness, they crucified Jesus. Some selfishly refuse to see the supply of love, patience, and mercy given to them through Christ as also being supplied for others. They choose not to extend or share that which he has supplied to cover ALL, a multitude of sins. I guess they get a high off the lie that they are more worthy and in doing so refuse to extend grace to those who appear not to be. But God moves

through love. So many of my associates, family, and brothers/ sisters in Christ tend to forget our true day to day purpose. We get so stuck on looking at a person's downfall that we miss the true

opportunity to extend a hand to help them up. This is true ministry during a spiritual warfare that

continuously goes on beyond the church's four walls. True love is shown through actions, not by words alone. It's truly a shame that during the times you need it the most, because of

whatever reason or preconceived notions, the support gets hindered and you get neither
action nor words. The Bible says we fight not against flesh and blood but against spiritual forces and principalities in high places. If one of your spiritual brethren or, for goodness sake, your real
brethren or flesh and blood has fallen - or is showing weakness on the battlefield - don't despise him or her, desert them, shake your head, or kick them while they are down. What does that say about you? You can fit your mouth to talk about them before you will open your mouth to pray or speak life to them. I have no respect for that. How is it that you seek to save the world, but you desire not to help the one who has fallen near your feet?

Just because a person doesn't respond the same way you do or refuses to go through the theatricals and dramatics of a situation doesn't mean that they don't care. With prayer, wisdom, and maturity, you can be graced with a peace that passeth all understanding. The carnal eye may read you wrong. But, when you really put on the full armor of God, you are protected, knowing that the weapons of warfare are not carnal. When you walk with him, he will provide you a peace that surpasseth all understanding.

Everybody may not understand or "get" you, baby, and that's okay.

God has assigned his angels and affirming vessels along the way. The spirit knows the spirit.

Differences

Opinions

Opinion is the medium between knowledge and ignorance. It is relative to one's perception not fact. Be open to the views of others, but always stand in your truth as you know it. As life changes, so do we, and so do others and opinions. So, in all thy getting, get understanding in your process. Honor you by following your heart, but above all else, make sure your heart is right by honoring God. Pray not only his will for your life but also for the lives of those around you. As long as you've gone before him and you're at peace, leave others and their opinions where they need to be, amongst themselves and none of your business.

Sleep...

Just because you sleep on somebody doesn't mean they're asleep. Just because YOU don't see potential doesn't mean there isn't any. Stop underestimating people. You are not the end all, say all nor are you God. You may not know what God is doing in the life of another or what His purpose is for that person.

There is always light in the darkness. If not, then YOU should be it instead of counting it all as lost and throwing out the good with the bad. Check yourself. One day to Him, we'll have to answer for the souls we easily prejudged and negated as unworthy, a waste of time, or too high of a cost amongst the least of these. There are many ways one can be poor beyond financial means and there are many ways we, who are rich in the fruits of the spirit, can be of positive influence. In my times of devastation and brokenness, I can clearly recall those who sustained my light by speaking life into me. I will forever sow seeds of faith, love, and hope to whomever God allows to cross my path You never know who you may be entertaining.

free

Give people time! You don't know what they may be fighting generationally.

Yes, everyone travels their own journey, but let's be real. When it comes to the hands we're dealt, pathology plays a huge part in the deal. Some people are truly fighting an unseen, but very evident, war waged long before them that they didn't even bargain for! But, now, it's their time to hold the sword to slay dark forces and strongholds in the name of the Lord. By his power given unto thee, a place of constant surrender and a high level of required sensitivity. In order to break, heal, deliver, release, and usher this mantle of family into a place of eminent liberty to bring into fruition those things requested by faith from those who've gone before and fulfill great grandma's pending declarations and promises of the Lord. Free. Redemption draws nigh.

Hypocrisy

When you don't practice what you preach, it sets the stage for confusion, mediocrity, and a lack of respect. I know that none of us are perfect, and we all fail at times to uphold the values we claim. But one thing that irks me is when people talk bad or knock someone else down for an expectation or behavior that they themselves do not practice or fail to live by.

"Judge and ye shall be judged". A lot of you self-righteous folks still don't get it.

Above All

I love how God moves behind the scenes, above all human understanding and beyond the expected. He uses who he chooses, not based on man's approval, and he reveals his spirit to those who diligently seek him, granting discernment. For the spirit knows the spirit, some accept while others defy; but, no matter how hard you try, you cannot deny His anointed. It's who He has appointed.

Sometimes you have to take a moment to get in alignment and rise so high in your vision that you don't allow anyone to define it or keep you stuck at a level defying your ambition. Share your energy with those who show mutual love, support, and belief in maximized potential - honoring your mission.

Trailblazer Writing

When "travailing" uncharted territory, have grace for those who are with you yet may not fully understand or know how to distinctly support or labor with you:

#1 - Understand Moses. Although you may go before them, they are still laboring too in their own bondage, oppression, and are pressing with you in the desire for the win. They may not understand it all now, but if they're of the same remnant, eventually they will.

#2 – What's in your hand? God needs you to come up higher above the murmur and above the noise, so he can reveal his vision and his plan without the crippling effects of distraction. He needs you to know that He and He alone is your source. He will create a way when there appears to be no way. It goes beyond your eyes. So overall, trust that, step-by-step, He will provide.

Going Through

We all have life lessons to learn; each of us on our own journey. At times, it can be very hard to watch a loved one go through. There may be times when I'm up and you're down, or you're up and I'm down.

Times that you're not burdened or going through a storm, but those around you are. Some people use those moments to make themselves feel "superior" or to pity others in the sense of a Pharisee, to kick someone while they're down. In those times, ask God to give you strength, to encompass you with his spirit to be a guiding light, and a reflection of his love. Be careful not to allow the enemy to use you in another person's situation, hang up, or downfall. Don't withdraw, press in. If you have nothing to give or say, speak life, press forward on their behalf through intercessory prayer and view it as an opportunity for direct ministry. Find your way of blessing and serve there.

Remember, when we get frustrated and feel powerless, He is powerful.

Soft river. Smooth force. Sometimes calm in chaos is a superpower. Match hate with love, negative with positive, betrayal with integrity, meanness with kindness, unpleasant with pleasant, and so on. Be intentional workers of good, not workers of iniquity.

Others

Some people show their ignorance by assuming the ignorance of others. Underestimating is an illusional tool for fools that leads to eventual defeat. Your pride and folly blind you to the point that you cannot see. But that which you sow, you shall one day reap.

So, be careful with whom you try to cheat, because life keeps track of all receipts.

Givers

It never ceases to amaze me. The miles you're willing to go for people compared to the inches they refuse to go for you. And they wonder why you stay blessed? Because you stay blessing others out of a pure heart, not grudgingly or out of evil motives, but simply because you care. Yet, I still say it's better to give than to receive. The giver will always have. The receiver will always need again, and the selfish always end up standing alone in the end. Sit back and watch. Life will break you down and take you through whatever hurdles you need to go through until you learn to appreciate the people, opportunities, and things God has placed before you.

Box

Don't waste your time attempting to define or put me in a box. You'll be in for a shock.

I'm still growing, so I'm not fully known. You did not create me, so you don't know the in's and out's, or what this girl or my purpose is all about. My life is full of favor and oxymorons. You'll run yourself amuck trying to have it all make sense, but allow me to give you a hint.

I'm not perfect. When I fall, I repent; I seek the face of the one by whom I've been sent.

So, as you're checking my dents while trying to cover your litter, make sure you correct your lies and call me the Truth Spitta.

god
is
good

God is good all the time, even if His timing doesn't reflect
mine. I'm learning to trust the process.

It's amazing that God can woo you back to purpose even in
the middle of your mess.

How He comes in and saves the day by sharing His higher
thought, showing me a better way, and

reassuring me that all will be okay. He is the hope at the end
of my rope.

He is the "yes" inside my "no". Put full confidence in Him; if
you don't, you should.

Because God is good all the time, and all the time God is
good.

Never Alone

Stepped outside to grab something out of my car. As I headed
back into the house, I stopped to turn around as something
grabbed my attention, but I can't say exactly what. I felt the
wind
blowing. I heard the trees clapping. I looked up to see the
stars winking at me. In that moment, without a single soul in
sight, I felt a sense of natural security and a reminder that we
are far from alone, even after death do us part.

There are times I lose focus, get distracted in the moment,
and temporarily losing sight of who I truly am. That's the
human in me. But oh, when I remember. I used to let it get
me down. Now, I know it's necessary levels to this journey. I
observe and embrace every step of this race.
Nevertheless, we both know whose I am. Sometimes numb bet
never sleep. Play with it if you want.

Protected

Straddling

Turning points happen when you decide. Don't straddle the fence. You devalue yourself and your time. Be decisive. There is so much power in decision. Give your opinion, know your voice, let it be heard, and don't give your power away. Connect, but don't allow yourself to be enmeshed in another so much so that you lose your own identity.

Culture

In some arenas   it's beautiful. In others, it's ghetto. In all areas, it's my culture. As far as I'm concerned, I'm not Pinocchio and you're not Gepetto. Not my master, nor creator. No, you don't pull no strings. It's my freedom of expression - the right to do my thing.

All things

You are not all things and neither should you have to be. You are you. You are a person with real feelings, real desires, limitations, wants, needs, and boundaries that deserve to be honored. Be okay with that, the pretty and the ugly. The kind and the not so loving. The truth, comforting, and the discomfort. The calm and the storm.

Shackles

Kings and Queens, no longer being held by visible shackles on
their feet but by shackles now
limiting their mentality.

Inferior

In order to restore a sense of pride in our culture, we must
first consciously reject and overcome a suppressed inferiority
complex created by hand-me-down thoughts or stereotypes fed
to us
throughout history in the media, music, news, schools, etc.
When we educate ourselves on our
own culture and history, far before the cotton fields and slave
trade, then we will be able to embrace the fullness of our whole
truth as a people instead of living, accepting, or adapting to
another culture's lies of a shameful, weak, ignorant, helpless,
and begging people. Just because they feed it to you doesn't
mean you've got to take it. When you know who you really are,
you stand tall. No one can break your stride nor steal your
pride.

Black

Man

Hated amongst many for reasons untold.

Treated like an animal, unwanted property - like you don't

possess a God-given soul.

Your past and present experiences, new and old, over time

has been cruel and cold.

Deception has fallen upon the masses....

However, I refuse to fold.

I will forever honor your treasure within you, as I myself was

birthed in your gold.

You, my King, produce beautiful sights to behold.

I pray for your peace and strength, that I may help you

to maintain your confidence and sanity, your hope for

humanity...and in the midst of calamity please know that you

will always fit this mold- designed to understand, comfort,

empower, and hold.

Nevertheless, do not cower Black Man.

Be bold. Be bold. Be bold.

You are awake. You are brilliant. You are free. You have the power to choose your perception - the way you see things. Will you choose to see the darkness or the light? Negative? Positive?

Choose to live in the now. Reject regret and take full advantage of today's opportunities. Your life is waiting on you. Go GET IT!

Please let us be careful not to forget to FORGIVE and PURIFY our hearts.

Not to allow seeds of fear, hate, and bitterness to take root in our hearts from acts of racism, hurt, betrayal, envy, or discrimination. You have to lay those feelings of hurt, anger, and betrayal before God. He knows the world that we are living in is full of hate and sin. Don't try to carry it. Also, being angry and rejecting him won't get you very far either, just years of confusion and stagnancy. Trust me. I'm speaking from very personal experience with

God, what I know. Please be careful and purify because if you don't you will begin to reflect that same hindrance. Don't allow another's hate to hold you hostage, to keep you from giving and receiving love.

If you allow this bitterness to take root, you will limit your capacity to theirs. Please be cognizant of this. It is infectious. What you see is what you'll continuously attract. Trust me, there are beautiful beings out there who are evolved in spirit; who are mature enough to see beyond cultural differences, who understand what it is to love, build, learn, and conquer beyond the perceived limit of skin color. If these are the people we aim to be and desire to be around, we must be able to maintain ourselves by exuding that exact energy vs the lower energies your perpetrator embodies.

TWe are not victims;
we are victors in a
world of chaos. Those
who embody hate are
the ones with the "disease" because they lack the fullness of
love. I am not speaking black versus white because I have
experienced ill treatment from both sides based on stereotypes
and assumptions. I am speaking beyond deceptive human
conditions and of love versus hate. Come up a little higher;
don't take the bait.

Feel it, process it, let it flow and know that you will be okay.
You are strong enough to journey with you through the tough
times. Don't look for an escape or act out self-destructively.
Be still, feel, and adjust accordingly. Self-awareness is
everything. Don't stunt your growth.
It will all work out beautifully this way. I promise.

Even in the times when you don't know what to do or lack the
words to say, honor your strength to stand. Value your effort
in showing up for yourself, in your willpower to BE, to rise
up in the midst of adversity.

Do your work. Stay in your lane. Focus on you, the most high,
and fulfilling the purpose you bring.
Don't be distracted. What may appear to be a shortcut can put

you off track for years. You know where you are and what it takes to get where you need to be. Stay the course, and it will all work out in perfect timing. Keep it moving. You are still on schedule. God has given you protection, provision, and potential that is developing and will manifest in due season. Do not abort your seed in frustration, uncertainty, or impatience. Rest in faith knowing that He is not a man that He should lie. As long as you are willing, trusting, and surrendering, He will complete the work He began in you. Yes, it's a process, but be confident in this & let God do His thing.

To my
Brother...

Some mornings, I find myself moving slower when my heart
and my mind are heavy, and I just need a few moments to
pause and be alone with me. Yet the world around me is
moving vastly. Reality has placed its demands on me. But I
want to go back, back to a time when you were here with me,
when pure innocence ruled our hearts and mind. We played,
we laughed, and felt free with time. Secured with the smell
of Big Ma's cooking in the early morning, amused by daddy's
jokes, fun-filled summers in Miami with Mema and Papa, and
singing in the choir trying to remember our notes. I know the
world is broken, but my heart bleeds all the more because you
were mine. And although I rejoice in good times, my heart
feels and my eyes do see that you're not by my side. I try to
hold it inside, but my love for you exceeds my pride.
I look at my niece in her eyes, and I recall how this cycle
deprives. I see me. I see you. I see, P. I'm working with
youth every day, trying to help them see life in a better way;
I carry you, your truth, your dreams, your voice with me.
Remembering you singing Dru Hill on repeat, popcorn was

all you'd eat, watching Dragon Ball Z everyday of the week, and doing your Taekwondo moves on me. Remembering all you loved and wanted to be. I see my nephews; I see my son - their lives have just begun. I swear to you with everything within me, I'll try my hardest to make sure their race is won.

But we all know there's this thing called "free will" and sometimes our choices can result in ill deals. And so I pray that you are able to see that even through the good and the bad, you are still ministry. I love you, bro.

We as humans are not, cannot, and will never be exempt from pain as long as we are human and living this journey. So, don't ever think that when you get fame, the man, riches, etc. that you are somehow exempt, and life struggles will come to an end. It actually only amplifies it. But when it does, readjust your perception and find comfort when the dark shows up. Don't identify with it; instead be the light for yourself and for others. You'll get through it easier.

Cycles

I talk to my children about generational curses and tools of
combat regularly.

Understanding that denial begets continual dysfunction while
awareness fuels the possibility for change, and the very act of
transparency empowers by removing scales from the eyes.

There is no room for lies. Truth causes freedom to rise.

Wounds

Wounds can be a window for light and healing - an
opportunity to learn, minister, and change or a wound can be
uncared for allowing infection to set in harvesting bitterness
and ongoing pain.

It all depends on how you protect or neglect it.

Absence

How do you overcome the need, want, and longing for an
absent or inactive parent's love?

The lack of manifests itself in many ways. When a parent
doesn't value a child, it messes up the child's values. The child
is left lost and meandering often searching for validation and
placing the power to do so in others' hands, when it is not
their responsibility to fill.

Secret Place

God is so capable of meeting you in that secret place, in what may seem to be one of your darkest hours, to overtake you with his love, healing, and restorative presence. To defy and expose the works of the enemy. To clarify any confusion, redefine all misconceptions, and direct you in the prosperous way of manifesting his will and strategic plan. Will you be fully present and in complete surrender?

Whispers

Earthen vessels have failed you. Great has been your disappointment; heavy has been thy load. But hear ye - I shall deliver you from underneath this bondage into the hands of one who will not just love you how you want to be loved, but love you as you need to be loved in ways you have never known or thought of.

Be still, my child. Deliverance is yours.

father
healing

Recognizing the unblemished love of a real father. Seeking to
define that which wasn't given. I no longer choose to reject my
healing. Fulfilling the empty spaces by choosing to show myself
a love I did not know. Not punishing myself, discrediting my
worth, or underestimating my value; I know that it's not my
fault. Little by little, I free myself from being held hostage
by the many things I was not taught like honor, respect, how
it feels to protect, when it comes to men what to expect, and
building the muscle of my inner beauty to be its best.

For so long, I've viewed men through the eyes of a broken
daughter expecting failure: the lack of trust, betrayal,
abandonment, desperateness, and neglect stuck on repeat.
The constant longing and denying, seeking to validate the
little girl within me. Sometimes giving up too soon; other
times holding on too long. In all my relations, I'm seeking
to right his wrong. I pull and push away, never satisfied -
deemed incomplete. It is only in the heavenly father's arms
that I can find sweet relief. Like helplessly chasing a feather in
the wind, these self-defeating beliefs must come to an end.

Day by day, He's showing me the love of a father, how to trust, and what love truly means. Uncovering and healing those places that are too deep for any man to have known or vaguely touch. He's making me whole, and it means so much.

To love and be loved is the notion, understanding that I am love and I am loved rather in the presence or absence of; it's my devotion.

Choices

Life is the total sum of your decisions. We enter in on the
decided path of those who came before us, observing and
conditioned for choice to decide on our own.

Every day, every situation is different. Some may be easy;
others are tricky. No one comes here knowing it all, those
who think they do are thrown curveballs and have unforeseen
falls. We can never completely control the future. We aren't all
knowing, but we can control what we choose and those choices
will no doubt effect our now and tomorrow. Choose wisely...

Ava

That was her name.

No one knew about her. She was buried in shame.

Bone of my bone, flesh of my flesh. How could I disdain?

Selfish of me; I couldn't see beyond my own pain.

Thinking with my emotions refusing to use my brain.

While I struggled with regret, daddy took you and wrapped
you in a teddy,

signifying even then we couldn't let go.

Deep down, you were loved and wanted.

We just wasn't ready.

And the memories remain.

Although you never took a breath,

one night my spirit filled with joy and instantly out of the
blue, I knew your name.

Ava, precious Ava, I will never be the same.

Catapult

Some situations and life lessons are painful, so much so that the lasting effects change the heart, shift the perspective, and catapult you into another dimension of existence. I mean falling so hard in a way in which you cannot save yourself, in a way that ONLY the Father's hands can catch you. When He does, you'll know it as it causes you to value the sanctity of life and uplifts you in a way that ensures you will never return to your vomit. The promise is, you are His. He will never leave you nor forsake you. Trust, His word will not return void. Set your love and focus upon Him. This is deliverance.

This too is a blessing.

forgive
Yourself

Forgive yourself as a mother, sister, daughter and friend;
For the times you dropped the ball and took an unforeseen
loss that looked like a clear cut path to a win.

Tears

Drowning in my tears I can't let them flow, fighting to hold on
to my pride.

I can't let these tears show; moving on, I've got to go.

Against my wishes as you know.

Grief Calling

When I talk to you, I feel grief....like something dead calling
my name.

I feel loved loss, the weight of sadness, the reminder that
there is nothing here to gain.

The voice that once brought joy is now a source of pain, and
although life has moved on the memory has left its stain.

Tears may fall, but there is a wall.

There will be no crossing, no trespassing at all.

I'm trying my best to move forth, but when faced with you,
those moments of reality stake their claim.

So please, I ask thee, let this distance remain.... understand
respectably, it's what I need to maintain.

Exhaustion Writing

If I'm truly being honest, I'm starting to feel disconnected from myself. Or should I say I am coming in to an awareness of the ways I have been denying me- mostly in part of sacrificing myself for others and not recognizing it as that, nor how to balance it. Life feels heavy. I feel a lot of hopelessness these days. Like I let my life slip through my hands behind stupid stuff and careless people. I feel a sadness and somewhat bitterness trying to overtake me. Sometimes I feel punished. To think, dream, or hope for anything differently feels tiring and out of grasp for my reality. I feel like I've been living in a fantasy world of faith and hope, and reality has finally awakened me. But I keep laying here trying to go back to sleep, to dream - because the noise, the hurt, and the weight of it all is just too much to carry.

I'm trying to reach high - to be creative, to live, to thrive - but my life seems so full of the mini issues and simple things that bog me down and occupy my time and attention so much so that I can't even begin to do anything nor fully accomplish the things I set out to do. It's too many things to constantly tend to, and I'm exhausted.

It is so important to remember this. I often find myself running on empty and trying to manage the various operations in my life. We and He knows all the things we carry externally and internally. I am having to learn to breathe. Surrender. And renew. It's the only way to gracefully make it through. We can't pour into anybody with an empty cup. It is crucial to ensure that we ourselves are full and replenished.

Self-care is everything!

Take a moment today and tend to the garden of your life, the matters of your heart, and to love on you.

You deserve it.

Self Care.

Healing
Writing

When you've seen brokenness on repeat your entire life so much that it has become a despised norm, a usual dysfunction that you may have even had a hand in while trying to escape, find your way or create something different. It's not always easy not knowing how and lacking the tools to build something new while trying to heal wounds and broken pieces all at the same time.

Begin to ask God to show you those things you thought impossible as possible through other people so that you yourself can begin to manifest it. You have to be receptive though you cannot allow envy, jealousy, past pain, regrets, shame, blame, self-limiting beliefs, distractions, or current dysfunction to get in the way. You must clear these things at his feet. It's a balancing act. Know that prayer, cleansing, and active visualization are so powerful.

Young, Single
Mothers
Writing

I became a mother before I became a woman. For so long, I beat myself up and discounted myself as invaluable and weak because I was underdeveloped as a woman. That's where the true imbalance came in. Males not rising up to play their part only further plummets the weight of responsibility, the support shared in parental love, and validation of worthiness on both levels. It all correlates hand in hand, but don't get it misconstrued. It takes a strong woman to be a great mother especially in the absence of these things, yet still coupled with the task of developing herself, her family, and her future.

Hopes deferred, crashing dreams, broken hearts, hidden tears, sleepless nights, and endless sacrifice, She deserves the crown.

Never should a woman be deemed weak, useless, or invaluable because she is a young mother, or a single mother. The truth of the matter is almost every woman aspires to be a mother.

This is the true essence and distinct ability in being a woman. The power to create and bring life force energy into existence. Where is the shame in motherhood? It's a lie from hell. Something that has been so shunned has to begin to be glorified in order to embrace women, fatherhood, childhood, parenting, and ultimately our world.

This idea that young mothers, or single mothers are undeserving and the lowest of the low is bull-crap; they are the strongest of the strong.

They have to embody the weight of two roles in one and constantly muster the strength to carry on.

Pure

Pure excellence. Purity in thought. In words, in deed, in
all things. Be intentional, especially in dealings with your
children. Those closest to you. Those who shall one day
rise up and call you blessed. Address the foul thing - the
unconventional, impure behavior. Children's spirits are pure
and untainted. Show them different, that sustained purity
is possible. Purity is beautiful; purity is light that glows so
differently like a light upon a hill.
For this too is a mere moment in time to make a lasting
impression on their pure minds.
Cherish this place. Honor that space.

How

How can I love you and continually show you that God is
love?
How can I consistently light up your world and cause you to
look above?
In curiosity, in wonder, and in love.

Voice

The skill of expressing how you feel. A lot of children are not taught or even encouraged to possess the skill of effective communication. Being raised in an environment where you abide only, not having a voice, and questioning why can be viewed as disrespectful or suspicious disobedience. So, the child internalizes the idea or belief that they have no voice or that their voice doesn't matter. Teach your children to operate in their voice and take pride in their voice as one of the most powerful gifts they can grant themselves. This is the vehicle in which they'll use to move through life in order to express who they are, their feelings, and their curiosity. Teach them how to use their voice in respectful yet firm and tactful ways. When a child knows the power, depth and meaning of their voice and that their voice matters; when they know they are heard, they will feel respected along with a sense of security and acceptance. They will feel validated. They will feel at home in their own skin and loved genuinely by being able to fully express what they hold within. Listen.

Pump your breaks and understand: before I am a mother or any other title, I'm a woman and behind this woman is a girl trying to make her way through life with the simple desire to love and

be loved. I am not super human; my life is made up of both beautiful and ugly moments. Being a full time mommy does not change that nor make it any easier. It only makes the moments more

worth the living. So, when it comes to parenting, I refuse to allow one who has not matched my effort and has the luxury to choose when they want to put time, money, or interest in yet chooses to do nothing or the very minimum to dictate when I have my moments or criticize my duty as a mother.

Man up or shut up because I'm running this.

The show goes on with or without your excuses.

Deuces.

Steps of a Mother

To love my children out of the joy of pure love - not shadowed by guilt, fear, or shame inflicted upon self or views of others that seek to discredit for many different reasons and "lack of". Do these things make a life any less valuable or undeserving in its pursuit of happiness?

I'd rather choose to focus on the wonderful opportunity to extend faith, hope, and love to a life that can only be given by God above. A great responsibility; I choose to further goodness in the world through my efforts of pure love unto the lives I am the head of. Infused by this power, I am humbly transformed. Finding it an honor instead of a burden, I pride myself in this role, unashamedly, with the good and the bad. Daily, I find myself stepping up to the plate with the courage to swing life's bat again and again. Knowing that my efforts are not in vain is like losing a game now and winning the championship later. I understand that all is necessary to advance my team. The beauty of recognizing what you truly hold in your hands. I do so relentlessly. Thank you, God for blessing me. I once held my head down, but now that it is lifted, I can finally see the strength that is found in being me.

To My Mothers

Just up thinking, and I realized something when I looked into my daughter's eyes. When I hurt, she hurts. When she hurts, I hurt. It hurts to see someone that you love and truly want the best for hurt. So with that being said, I just want to say a simple thank you to the mothers of my life who have been there for every call, listened to me wallow, and reminded me of who I am by encouraging me through countless hours with words of wisdom.

I heard fierceness and hurt in your voices on behalf of some of the things I was going through very loud and clear. Just like I love and want the best for my little girl - you want the best for me.

I respect that. I am only standing on the strength of your shoulders right now. I thank God for providing me with you. I'm sorry for every dishonorable act, word, or way that I have hurt you, discounted you, or shunned the love and time you have invested in me while on this journey. Sometimes, I really think I know it all or I'm just gung-ho on learning it my way

through my own falls, discrediting your shared experiences and attempts to catch me. I know who is in my corner now and who has always been, no matter what yesterday held.

I love you. I appreciate you. I honor you.

Self-Motivation

I think the best thing for me to do is get focused and motivated about the betterment of me and my kids. Although it feels life threatening, it's really not. It's only as threatening as I allow it to be. It only has the space, strength, pull, and power that I allow. It's time that I rise up, direct, and take control now. Minimize those things that don't speak truth towards success, quality, and potential in our future. Those things that tear down the spirit and the very essence of life itself instead of building it up. This requires a paradigm shift and a different mindset that has to be consistent in the focus upon overcoming the challenges that will bring about mental, physical, emotional, and spiritual change.

The power is truly in your hands.

You have to decide and act. Don't lose hope. Where there is life, there is hope and this alone defies the illusion of death - or what "seems" to be the end. You will rise again.

Careful

Be careful and concerned about who, what, and where you allow yourself and children to be vulnerable; this is how they interpret power through weakness and strength.

Be careful what you show kids because they will remember.

Your actions, words, and situations may expire, but by memory they will always be able to tap into it and relive it over and over again. It will overall effect the lens in which they view themselves, others, life, and even God. So be mindful and create great memories. Let it be inspirational. But, in the not so good memories, intentionally make it right by making it a teachable moment.

Life Goes On...

While I am pregnant, you have left me deserted, ignored, and neglected while you seek to build something with someone else. I have never felt pain like this before. It resembles the rejection and feelings of abandonment I've felt from my father. When all I ever wanted was
to love him and be loved. Yet, all I can do is smile while tears roll down. I wait for better days to come. I can no longer fear that which has already been done. It says a lot about the person you truly are, and I choose to no longer fight it but accept it and move on because as you have so ruthlessly shown, life goes on.

Everything is Everything

Don't hold yourself captive; let it go, baby girl. There's joy, peace, and love waiting for you on the other side of that fear. Shift your focus from that which appears to be a loss and step forward in faith. Of all there is to gain,
everything is everything.

High Road

It's amazing to me how much better you are able to coast through a perceived bad time by reassuring yourself of God's endless love - a consistent, powerful source always there ready and waiting for you.

It truly shifts your focus to your endless potential and possibilities to not get caught up in an illusion but to envision, create, and maintain the mindset from which you desire to be manifested. Refuse to criticize.

I repeat: refuse to criticize, be angry, or consumed with negativity towards another. Simply release these types of people or sources of relations that refuse to positively align but rather encourage these negative reactions within you. By continuing attachment, you harbor unforgiveness and find temporary moments of motivation based on false means. You are then left feeling stuck and powerless. Instead extend grace and let go without the daunting crazy up and down task of trying to control that which you cannot, ANOTHER. Wasted energy taken away from you and your forward motion. Do not give your power away; deposit it wisely on what will be a sure return of your greatest investment, my love, YOU.

Choose to take the HIGH road; you don't have to walk down anybody's back alley.

To Win

I pray to God that I will never again fall in love, invest my time, energy, and life into someone who has no intention on loving me or my children. The pain and heartbreak that follows this illusion of being "unlovable" is just too real. I can no longer allow my family to be open to heartbreaks on behalf of my inability to choose or recognize true quality.

By following my hopes and desires, their hearts are placed on the line too.

I can't risk them breaking anymore. In addition, I've brought another life into this cycle.

When will this memory end? I feel like I lack the tools and set of skills that it takes to successfully win, when all I want is to love and be loved.

I never imagined it would be this hard to gain or that in receiving something so natural as love it would feel like endless loss and ongoing pain.

Love yourself and your current/future children enough not to entertain or allow in your space men who lack the qualities of a husband, father, and a lifetime mate.

Wonder

Have you ever wanted to believe in the beauty of love, but
the ugliness robs you of your confidence? Have you ever
wanted to bask in its warmth and solitude, yet the burdening
stories of broken hearts of people who took that lovely fall
and ended up losing it all constantly serve as a reminder that
relationships are a risk?

That heartfelt passions can be temporary bliss, and so I'm
tangled in the midst of joy and pain, loss and gain, honor or
defeat at the road where my fear and faith meet?

What shall it be?

Cowards

It amazes me with some guys the main things they admire the woman for are her strength and dignity, which are the same things, once he's got her, he will use against her as his excuse and crutch. If you're not ready, leave that woman alone, cause, in the end, her strength will expose your weakness as a supposed man. A crack her heart didn't have to heal if you would stop the perpetrating, knowing you ain't bout nothing for real. The inability to sincerely give love and trust reflects cowardliness. The ability to open up your heart to love and trust not based upon selfish gain shows courage and strength. "And now these remain - faith, hope, and love - and the greatest of these is LOVE." 1 Corinthians 13:13.

Quality requires quality. You've got to put in work, effort, and tenacity. If you aren't willing to give of yourself, then tell me why should it be yours? If you have the vision but refuse to honor your passions with action, how do you expect it to manifest? It won't. Life simply doesn't work that way. Come up a lil higher or continuously choose to repel that which is greater.

Love Known

You said you love me, but how would I know it? Tell me, what is love if you never show it? A love known is a love shown.

A Flower

Understand that before she is anything else, She is a woman who flourishes with the desire, the want, the need to be loved and accepted; not weakened by being neglected, ignored, or rejected. Your unethical absence leads her right into the appreciation of another's presence. She WILL be loved. For only so long can she go on with her seeds of love not being sown, or the lack of it being shown but instead thrown back in her face. It has to be pruned and grown so that it may go on; this is the survival of a woman. She is like a flower. Don't think for a moment that because you refuse to care she has to lay withered there. Nourishment will soon come and like a flower she will not refuse water. What you won't do, another one will. The lack there of makes my desire even stronger to be fulfilled. The absence of your arms led me into the extended arms of another. You are who I want; however, you chose not to provide for me. Sometimes a fresh start is the only thing that soothes a panicking heart.

Honor Thyself

I want someone who can see, love, honor, and caress the woman in me. That's something the boy in you doesn't know how to do, yet it's also a reflection of me. If I knew how to honor myself, with you I would not have chosen to be.

This Moment

It's okay. As much as it hurts, I'm going to allow myself to experience the joy and pain in this loneliness tonight. It is the subtotal of codependency, and all that I have done and failed to do up to this moment. This is, however, never my lasting reality, but just a moment in time to reveal the reality of toxicity within myself and another.

Talk is cheap and time is money. I never truly understood what that meant until I spent time and wasted energy with a man who was bent on selling dreams that resulted in harsh realities.

Holding Writing

I'm trying to hang on, but truthfully I feel like I'm the only one doing the holding. Yeah, you do your part as far as your child because that was chosen. But deep down a part of me is Sad, silently still unfilled. I know there is no such thing as a perfect love, yet I'm yearning still. It's like I'm giving all of me while you're getting all of you, but I'm losing me trying to maintain. School work behind, not paying bills on time, five days no sex, not even a cuddle. I think I want to rebuttal. I don't mind a promising sacrifice, but in the meantime at least a WCW would be nice. I know it's not all about me, but at least show me it's not all about you. We still have love to show and trust to prove. I want to be happy - no matter what the situation is in life. Happiness is what I thrive to live. There is a difference in being happy and content. I refuse to be content with unhappiness, especially when I've seen and experienced it at its best.

I rather be with someone whose love doesn't feel any less.

Distracted Terrain

It starts with being unfocused, resulting in losing vision of who you really are. So pleasurable is the rise to compromise. So lost in the comfort you can't quite find put your finger on the lies. However, you can feel them near and wishing it away or acting as if it doesn't exist won't make it disappear. But with no evidence, where do you go from here?

Wreck Yoself

...and I told her, "Girl, stress not; don't second guess your value nor allow yourself to compete. Let him wreck himself, and be happy you chose to get out of the passenger's seat."

Potential

It's not that you're not a good person. It's just that you're not all that you proclaim to be, and I'm tired of wishing, hoping, and waiting on your useless potentialities.

Wise enough to know what's worth fighting for and when to let go; or indecisively choosing defeat by holding on to a false sense of love and loyalty. Why drink lies from a cup that has expired when you can have a newfound fountain that flows with what you desire...

Expired

My
Addiction

I have an addiction. It is you.

Disguised

A beautiful fall, feeling so good, disguised as the perfect rise.
The best to ever glide through these thighs, a magician - I fell
for your tricks. But I will never sell my soul in exchange for a
dick. Realizing game ran on me; now, you ain't shit. I tried to
give you a chance, placed my esteem in your romance. Making
my exit, now you can no longer fuck my sanity. You gain
power in being deceitful, but the truth is you'll always end up
in defeat. Cause people will eventually come to their senses,
realigning defenses, and see past this facade of you.
Once again, you'll be left alone, waiting for your next victim
to come along, singing the same ol song. But you'll never get
it right doing wrong. People will eventually move on. So the
only one stuck in this pitiful process of losing is you. You
thought you dogged my senses, but not enough that I couldn't
see. Homie, you're not at all what you claim to be.

The Maze

There's so many highs & lows when it comes to you. I'm
confused in knowing what's false or true. Sitting here on
stuck. I don't know what to do. I don't want to be stuck on
stupid yet don't fully know how to move forward toward the
truth. But, what's true anyways?

Lost in this daze; I hate this phase - it's like a relational maze
of defeat.

Soul Snatcha

He's possessed with a spirit that has a need to devour.

Subduing you completely, rendering you helpless unto him is how he gains his power.

Minute by minute, hour by hour, he requires all your time and attention.

The physical pleasure is the best hands down without any other mention.

Realizing that this all along was the true intention. I'll never forget not long after we first met,

You asked if I thought one could surrender their soul during sex.

It had me perplexed, but I answered yes, not knowing that this all alone was your hex.

I thought you were really deep, but you was on some other shit.

Now, no matter how mad or done I am with you, I've got to have another hit.

But I can't, man, you're sick. You're the type to break a woman down and get high off of it.

But you ain't getting high off me no more.

I'll suffer in this longing; I'm not opening that door.

You're more than a coincidence.

You're a distraction, one that was strategically sent.

Must suck though, you didn't get to complete the purpose in which you were meant.

Now, you're powerless and all hell bent.

Don't know what to do or where to go;

don't dare look for me to grow your ego.

I already did enough of that, so hit the road jack.

I promise you - it ain't no coming back.

You see, every devil has its day to burn,

and I had a lesson to learn.

Don't play with fire, be cautious and contain your desire.

Because it alone can lead you down a path of no escape,

even though at first glance it may look great.

And like a roller coaster, there are those who are only here for the thrill on repeat.

Watching you scream, captivating you with lies that there is no other place to be.

But the truth is there is so much more to see.

You were a lesson taught through the journey of intuition, the act of finding truth in the face of fiction, the uncovering of what is shown and hidden. You taught me the consequence in apathetic ignorance. You flexed that muscle very well. Of all the stories my heart could tell, she'd give a gentle yet firm reminder unto that inner voice. Please listen because right in the thick of hot fantasies and a cold reality lies a very conscious intuition urging you over and over again to focus my love and pay attention.

Intuition.

A Collection of Hearts

You chose to ignore me when I told you I needed time to heal.

Now, you're looking at me sideways and treating me like I'm a bum deal.

You guys let lust rule your eyes, refusing to respect a woman trying to keep it real.

Say what you got to say, do what you must to play, and get yourself a feel.

It's funny how you get her the way you want and then the true you is revealed.

Adding insult to injury, fury to her pain.

As she lies deceived and hopeless - tell me what have you truly gained?

Perception

Sometimes I don't like the weakness or vulnerability that comes along with being in love...and at other times I enjoy it.
I think it's based on security. If you feel secure, you're good, but if for any reason, real or imagined, you feel the latter, it'll begin to make the heart heavy versus happy.
Then, I believe, you either create or confirm problems, which furthermore deepens insecurity.

No Convo

We'd sit on the phone for a very long time after discussing what we both did wrong.
In silence, without the words to say while not wanting to move on.

Over

My heart longs for you; I had to leave you behind.
I really wanted you to journey with me, but you're not of the
same mind.

So, we would've just fell behind in our paths to destiny,
struggling day to day with different viewpoints about which
way to go, to follow, and arguments about truth.

When, in all actuality, we are both standing stagnant not
making any beneficial moves.

We can't hold each other back any longer, I refuse.

I know you'll find your way, I had to follow mine.

I hope you know I love you; if not, you'll understand in time,
when you can appreciate the realness in honoring all parts
of you and the beauty found in journeying with a person who
does too.

Best wishes.

One Day

One day, you'll meet a girl, and you will love her dearly. She'll be enough to meet your needs; she'll be caring enough to heal your broken places and strong enough to tear down your wall.

She won't have to beg for flowers, compliments, or your attention.

You will honor and protect her heart as if it were your own.

You will give her your all.

I have come to accept that I am not her.

Unfortunately, you are not ready, and that's okay.

I loved you anyhow.

It hurts because I really wanted to trust you.

I really wanted to believe what you said.

But something kept holding me back.

Now behold, it has appeared in facts.

And although I was right about you, a part of me was hoping that I was wrong.

That's why, despite all my inner turmoil, I held on so long.

Released

Mistake

I made a mistake by loving too soon.

I made a mistake while still in half bloom.

I made a mistake; I should not have assumed.

I made a mistake; now all I have are blue moons.

You left me standing alone.

Yet still, in order to get past you, I must admit.

I made a mistake. I saw the red flags yet still traveled the

distance further into the unknown.

The yesterdays staring at today; reality full grown.

I made a mistake, and I must - I will correct it, all on my own.

Self-Loyalty

Getting lost within another...Not knowing where you begin or where they end, can be a WONDERful journey of highs where the two become one and combined you reach the sky. But at its worse, during times of betrayal or an unraveling reverse, it can be a survey of

lows - a place of risked vulnerability, a fight to reclaim the heart and sometimes your very soul.

Don't lose yourself, baby. Find and combine, but before you commit to build, be sure to count the cost. Evaluate all possible outcomes of the situation and consider every variable in the equation.

Never set yourself up for a loss. Secure yourself in a way that you will always remain a boss.

Understand one thing: My position will remain even if you change.

It's risky to fall, but you don't have to lose it all. I prefer to be lifted, no overcompensating - both mutually gifted. Not empty handed trying to recover in the name of a so called "lover."

new

Lane

I danced with fear, smooth how he snuck in

and grabbed my hands.

I thought with him I was protected.

So cunning, I should've rejected.

I've strolled with pain.

Going back and forth on who should be blamed until I

realized that revenge and bitterness are one in the same.

I let that hurt go; I'm moving in a new lane.

Got a phone call the other day from regret.

Heard I'm moving on and just wants to show his respect.

Left a long voicemail ending with the word "bet."

But I haven't even returned his phone call yet.

He holds me to a lot of things that I want to forget.

So, here I sit pondering where my energy should be invested.

My love has been tried and found true, post tested.

Reciprocating is a must, not a suggestion.

Femininity

Smooth love, care, and affection. Soft but firm - confident, self-assured, and loyal. Lioness. Sacred; protect this space. Allow yourself to recharge and rest in it. Claim it. Find your internal and external balance. And let no man, woman, vulture, violator, nor circumstance to harden you or influence you to perceive it as "weak". It is powerful. It is vital. It is necessary.

All hail Femininity.

Reclaim

I am sexy.

Rightfully in my skin.

Bursting from within.

I will not hang my head low feeling incapable, ashamed to express, or give all I have to show. Feelings of guilt about a natural pleasure because of what you stole.

I yearn to be free, deserving of love, and love deserving of me.

An honorable touch.

I want to celebrate my body; its well overdue. She's been sooo good to me: loving, patient, and healing. Please be gentle and patient with me as I get to know and am being reintroduced to valuing my body. Understand that my first experience with sex was not pleasurable. It was scary. It was fearful. It was robbery. I was robbed of me, my understanding, my innocence, my self image, and my identity.

I was used. It was a selfish act.

And I'm trying my hardest to come back from that.

Love is healing, fulfilling the emptiness. Be an active part in your partners healing. Don't run & despise the person when the infatuation fades & human flaws began to show. True love is healing, so is tough love; finding healing through forgiveness and letting go. Either way, love is always and will always be the answer. It's the force field God operates in.

healing love

When the love is real, so loud and reassuring that it drowns
out doubt and smothers all fear.
Loving every part of me, your love is freeing to my

insecurities. Resistance and pain
encounters defeat when my pain and
your pleasure meet.

More

What we have is all my trust level can allow. I want more.

my Love

My love is as mysterious as an unborn child. With the right nourishment, it can sink you as quick as quicksand, but the wrong negativity can push it away like the low tide of a full moon. I am a woman who needs and fiends for true love. And when I have found it, I will cherish it as God cherishes a marriage. The head of my life, the head of my kingdom to be that woman that controls my emotions and runs the empire like a true queen runs her dynasty.

My love is as deep as a dark summer night, wrapping you in its warmth as you permeate my very essence. Gazing, you see the stars twinkle in my eyes. You feel my passion flowing unto you as you go deep, loosing yourself and fulfilling your presence in me.

I Do

Went through "couple" things, ups and downs, growing pains, but one thing remains the same; regardless of who was to blame, love never changed. Tried and true, I dedicate my loyalty to you, to honor your last name.

I finally say, "Yes, I do. I love you."

The Beauty of Trust

A relationship with the mutual understanding that life can
been hard, yet still be able to enter into our sacred place
softened without the worry of scars. To lay our weapons down
and relax the walls around our guarded hearts. Genuinely,
in return, it provides a safe space for one another to be
free from the fear of vulnerability, assumed judgments, and
negativity, escaping the various pains and broken remains
by life's thieves. We heal in the rejuvenating power of one
another's capacity to dive deep into pure love and unfiltered
trust. Continuously rising; matured enough to know that to
truly embrace one, the other is a must.

Warriors of love, protecting all that is ours - defeating
anything that would cause us to stumble, cower, or cripple
the power we have found through one another. It's making
that final decision that there will be no other lover. Realizing
the reality of a true partnership. Commitment to you is
commitment to me; to love, life, vision, destiny, future, and
present dreams.

Coupled heart in hand, we fully understand what it
takes to stand the test of time. I won't betray yours and you
won't betray mine. Trust.

I Felt Love Today

I felt love today, and its presence was beautiful
tears of joy overflowing, a peace so serene amidst the deferred
hopes, broken hearts, and shattered dreams.
I felt love today by way of a helping hand, a listening ear, and
a shared strength to stand.
I felt love today through the warmth of your presence, the
glow in your smile, and reassurance in your voice that amidst
all the chaos, amongst all the noise, you are here by choice.
No, you didn't get ghost but remained true when I needed you
the most.

Yes, I felt love today, and I just want to say, Thank You.